LESSONS LEARNT

Diary of an ECT

Lauren Aldridge

DEDICATION

To my family and friends,
Thank you for all the support you have given
me on my teaching journey so far.

CONTENTS

PROLOGUE

Firstly, thank you for choosing my book and joining me to hear all about my lessons over the first two years of my teaching career. As part of the first cohort to go through the new Early Career Teacher (ECT) framework, I thought I could enlighten people with some of my ups and downs so far. It began with me simply writing down my reflections some days, I just wanted to get it out of my head and to revisit the day. However, I soon realised that perhaps my feelings and experiences could help others, and that's why I'm here.

This book is all about honesty and openness. My aim is to normalise the feelings you will likely experience in your first few years of teaching. I'm certain that most teachers' experiences would be similar to mine. I wanted to write this as a true reflection of my experience while also highlighting the positive aspects that far outweigh the difficult days.

I want to reach as many aspiring teachers as possible with this book so that you know you are not alone. I believe that other teachers and mentors can also benefit from understanding the emotions that Early Career Teachers (ECTs) go through. Some of these experiences may continue to arise as I progress in my teaching career, but discussing them is, in itself, uplifting.

I completely understand why they extended support to teachers for their first two years of teaching. It is challenging, and even though you have completed your training, there is still a lot to learn. I hope you will gain valuable insights from my lessons, as well as the advice and tips I provide along the way.

Allow me to share a bit of background on how I became a teacher. I met my husband at 17, and he later joined the army, initiating our journey of travel. I worked as a Learning Support Assistant (LSA) in Colchester before transitioning to become senior support worker in a care home for adults with autism. This was a challenging job, but I learnt a great deal and still implement many of the strategies I learnt there in my classroom today.

While working, I pursued a degree through The Open University in Health and Social Care, specialising in Children's wellbeing and Mental Health. At that point, my career goal was to become a social worker. Teaching was an option but not my primary ambition.

About six months later, we moved to Germany – a significant change that required me to venture into a completely new country without a job, friends, or family. Shortly after our move, my husband deployed for four months. This was an incredibly tough time, but I pushed through and managed to secure a position at a local Ministry of Defence School. I absolutely loved that job! I made numerous wonderful friends, both among my colleagues and the children. It may sound cliché, but it truly felt like one big family. To achieve my degree whilst working, I had to be disciplined, dedicating a few hours every night to studying and using weekends to write essays.

This is when I decided to change my career path and become a teacher. We spent four amazing years in Germany, where I adored my job, which inspired me to explore teaching further. Following this, we moved to Belfast. In Belfast, I was fortunate to secure a role as a Sensory Coordinator at a family adventure centre. I continued pursuing my degree whilst juggling work and family life. I truly enjoyed this job; I worked in the sensory room, providing support to families with children who had special needs. I completed a course and became an "Autism Champion" for the centre, creating tailored sessions for individuals with autism and organising sensory events. My understanding and experience with special needs grew during my time there and I was able to apply my previous knowledge to support the families. Unfortunately, the centre closed for two years due to the pandemic.

Since I loved that job so much, this closure served as the incentive for me to apply for teacher training. I had grown accustomed to waiting until we knew our next move before making any plans, so initially, I planned to wait until we returned to England to start my teacher training. However, as I was no longer working and couldn't pursue the same course in Northern Ireland, my husband encouraged me to commence my teacher training then.

This decision proved challenging, as we lived

apart for a year, and due to restrictions, neither of us could travel to see the other. Nevertheless, I enjoyed my year of teacher training and was grateful for the opportunity. I qualified in 2021 and began my first teaching job in the new school year. That's when my journey as an Early Career Teacher (ECT) began.

I am grateful for every step of my journey, as I have learnt a great deal and gained experiences I never thought possible. I feel that all of these experiences have made me a better teacher, and I wouldn't have it any other way. I have grown and changed significantly since leaving school, and I believe that my teaching journey would not have been the same if I had entered the profession immediately after graduation. Relocating and working various jobs taught me valuable skills and life lessons that have had a profound impact on my teaching, resilience, and self-discipline.

I sincerely hope that this book will help others and allow you to realise that your feelings are not unique. Furthermore, I hope to bring a few laughs by sharing some of the many funny and positive stories from my first two classes. I wouldn't have made it through my first two years without the support of my husband, family, friends, and all the children I have had the pleasure of teaching so far!

At the end of each chapter, I have included key takeaways. I find it helpful to recap the information I've read and see it presented in bullet points. Seeing information in a different format helps me remember, and I hope it will be beneficial if you need to revisit any of the topics I've discussed. Now that you know a bit about how I entered the teaching profession, I will proceed with my lessons learnt.

LESSON 1: NAVIGATING THE FIRST TERM ROLLERCOASTER: FINDING BALANCE AND PROCESSING NEW INFORMATION

I want to normalise the many emotions of a teacher. I am being completely honest when I say I cried a lot in my first term. After my first day, I cried all the way home! Don't get me wrong, I had a fantastic day. My school and my colleagues were great, but it was really overwhelming. When I reflected on the day and unpacked the amount of new information I had to absorb, I accepted that it was ok to feel like this. I was in a completely new environment, with people I had never met before. Even learning the route to my classroom felt overwhelming.

Usually the first few days of a school year are filled with training, which is great. It allows you a few days to get organised before the children start. But for a new teacher in a new school, this was an intense few days. So, just be prepared to take in a lot of information. I had two morning training sessions and the afternoons were free to sort out the classrooms and do some planning for the rest of the week. This was really helpful, but your brain does feel a bit frazzled, so make sure you make time for yourself those first few weeks in the evenings. It's okay to not expect too much of yourself; you would have been working so hard during the day.

My advice would be to make sure you have prepped some good nutritious meals to keep you going and to relieve some worry and time when you get home. You want to take time to relax and wind down after each day. It would be helpful to write down any thoughts from the days, clear your head a bit and make a list of what absolutely needs to be done before the children come. Sometimes you think you need to do so much but when you sit back and think about it, is it actually going to benefit the children's learning? Do I actually need this right now? I remember having a lot of brain fog the first week, so writing things down helped me to remember what I needed to do and take some pressure off my mind.

Make sure you get a good night's sleep that week. Teaching is exhausting, and I especially found my first few weeks very tiring. I mean, I still get very tired now and am often in bed by 9:30pm. I think that comes with the job. I read something before that said teachers have to make so many decisions in a day that it makes them physically exhausted. To take on such a big responsibility is hard work and I don't want to put you off but just give you a heads up that you might feel really tired so make plans around that too.

I think it's important, as it is with all professions, to accept that there will be good days and bad days. As I've said I cried a lot in my first term, but there was some really good days and you have to cherish these too. That's why I started writing things down at the end of the day, so I could reflect and clear my mind. This then led me to think, why not write a book and see if I can show other new teachers that these feelings are completely normal. This might not work for everyone; I know some people who can just switch off from the day once they've left work. If this works for you, then great! You just need to find a way to put the day/week behind you and enjoy time with yourself, family and friends.

As I am writing this, I am coming to the end of my second year. I have learnt what works for me at the end of the day. Most days, I don't write it down anymore; I tend to reflect in the car on the way home. I have been writing this book, which has given me opportunities to think about situations. As a teacher you will forever be reflecting on how lessons went, whether you would do it again like that or whether you need to switch up the following day to practise a concept more. You need to be adaptable and flexible. You also need to understand that not everything will go to plan. I have had many lessons where, in my head, it goes very differently to how it actually went; sometimes it goes better than you imagined.

The nerves I felt in my first term were crazy. I had a huge responsibility to teach, care for, safeguard and inspire a whole class of 5/6-year-olds. To go from your training year where you teach some lessons by yourself with your mentor in the room to having a classroom full of children to teach and an LSA with whom you are also responsible for directing is the most nerve-racking feeling. I can look back now and know that I did not need to be so worried. I am completely capable (and children are not that scary, neither was my LSA).

It turns out that most teachers feel like this, even experienced teachers that have worked for years and had many different classes. When I would bump into teachers at my school in the staffroom, we would talk about how it was going, and every teacher I spoke to was also nervous to meet their new class. Once I opened up about my worries to the staff at my school, I realised that I was not alone. Some of my friends from my teacher training also messaged about their worries and it was surprising to see that so many people felt the same.

My favourite part of my first week, Friday pub club! A few teachers from my school would meet in the pub most Fridays. It was just a nice time to have a catch-up and chat about our weeks. We could offload if we needed to and just share some highlights of the week. Although you are around a lot of people all day at work, you don't really get much time for adult conversations. So, this was a nice opportunity to meet some people at work and talk about our weekend plans. It was lovely to talk about all of the things we had to look forward to over the weekend and to switch off. By the Friday evening, I had stopped crying and my drive home was a little different than the days before.

Talking to family and friends, made me realise that not only teachers have these nerves when starting a new job; everyone does. I remember people reminding me that there are so many different parts to a new workplace – you're learning people's names, your navigating a new environment, you're learning new ways of doing things, new policies and procedures and trying to have a good work-life balance at the same time. I even started to question my career choice: is this right for me? I don't think I'm cut out for this. It was a really difficult time mentally, which is why I want to highlight this and share my experiences. But you need to give yourself a chance to settle in. Before I knew it, within a few days, I already felt more in control and happy about this fresh new start. You need to give yourself time.

Also, I hear a lot of trainee teachers asking what they need to buy for their first year. Please do not go out and spend your own money on things for the classroom. Of course, it's up to you, but you really don't need to. Schools have so many resources, and you don't really know what you'll need until you've looked at the curriculum, your planning and the needs of your class. Also, more than likely someone in school might have what you need, and you can borrow it rather than buying lots of things.

You won't really know what works for you until you've been in the job a few months. I brought all of this fancy stationery (yeah, it made me feel good and professional), but I didn't use half of it. I got this pad where you add your daily jobs, I used it for the first two days then I didn't use it anymore. I found it easier to add to electronic post-it notes on my computer. That way it was always there when I was doing planning on my laptop, and I couldn't lose it! I also found that tasks can extend over several weeks, so a daily list just didn't work for me.

Another thing I hear teachers buying a lot is books. I love reading, and I love a new book as much as anyone else. There are also some great stories out there for children. However, before you buy anything, have a good look around your school, ask other teachers, ask family and friends that have young children. Otherwise, I find that you end up with lots of books which you need to store somewhere (you don't want lots of books in your book corner; it's nice to rotate them) and when you move schools, you have a lot of books to pack up too. So, my advice would be, if you really love a story, then buy it, but otherwise try to borrow books or find an online read-aloud version, you can even find PDF versions of some books online. This is just a warning before you get into a spiral that lots of teachers do of buying books and running out of storage.

But, seriously, don't spend your whole summer before you start worrying about whether you've bought enough. This is time for you to relax and recuperate after a hard-working training year.

I have moved schools a couple of times since starting teaching. I moved in my second year to support my own well-being. I relocated much closer to home, which allowed me to save time on commuting. As a teacher, time is previous, and travelling 30-40 minutes each way, depending on traffic, was a significant portion of my day that I really wanted to reclaim. While there are many positives to my previous schools, I made this move for my well-being, and I can't wait to see what this new journey brings. Since I've started at a few different schools in September, I thought it would be helpful to create a first week checklist, focusing on the most important thing to know for getting through the initial week. Everything else can wait. At the end of this chapter, there is a simple checklist you can use to help you navigate the first week. In the following paragraphs, I will discuss a few things you might need to ask or think about.

Find out how to do the register. Ask someone to show you how the system works, where you find the lunch menu, and if visuals of the menu are needed for KS1. Determine whether the children or the parents make the lunch choices. Also, learn how to input the data into the system. Each school I've been in has had a different system, so if you can familiarise yourself before starting, it will be one less thing to worry about on your first day with the children. I remember my first year, realising suddenly that I didn't know how to do the register about 20 minutes before the children were due to come in. My mentor gave me a quick tour, but this was a panic I could have avoided, if I had checked this beforehand.

Next, get a diary or use an online calendar to record important dates, assemblies and meetings and other events you need to attend. If you have a staff weekly briefing, make sure you bring your diary as they usually discuss this week's agenda. Here's a top tip: when looking for important dates, check the school newsletter, as most schools include significant events in it.

Take the time to find out about your students. Hopefully, you will have the opportunity to speak with their previous teacher or, if you are in Early Years, review transition notes from the nursery. The first thing you need to find out is if any students have medical needs or allergies. I usually keep a list of this information in a folder on my desk. Also, find out if there are any students with special educational needs and disabilities (SEND). You might need to gather resources, such as fidget or sensory toys, and enlarge documents for students with visual impairment. Additionally, spend some time with the students during the first few days. I like to fill out a one-page profile with each child, discussing their likes, dislikes, preferred learning styles, and how they like to be supported. It's also great to have these profiles accessible in the classroom, so substitute teachers can refer to them.

Develop some behaviour strategies you will use in your classroom. Find a couple of attention-getters that you will use with your class. These will help ease transitions (there's a whole chapter on this later on). Also, come up with positive behaviour strategies that you will implement. Personally, I found Paul Dix's (2017) book, 'When the Adults Change, Everything Changes' to be a lifesaver for behaviour strategies. However, make sure you read the school's behaviour policy as well. There might be a whole school approach that you will need to adopt. Familiarise yourself with the system for managing behaviour and consequences in your school. It might helpful to print parts of the behaviour policy so that you have them on hand at the start of the year.

Read the safeguarding policy and make sure you know how to record information. There might be an online system for which you'll need a login. Being prepared for reporting incidents will help you feel calmer if something does happen. Check how your school records different types of incidents. In my current school, we record everything online in one system, including safeguarding, conversations with children that need to be documented, behaviour incidents, and conversations with parents.

In some schools, the first couple of inset days are focused on safeguarding as all staff need a yearly update. As a new member of staff, you'll likely need the initial training. Some schools might also discuss their behaviour policy. There's no harm in being prepared by reading through it beforehand and starting to think about how it will apply to your class.

Lastly, make sure you ask questions. Remember the saying, 'No question is a silly question', as it holds true. If you are unsure or worried about something, just ask. You will have a mentor whom you can turn to for guidance. In my first week, I remember asking questions all day long, and that's what mentors are there for – to support you. Other staff members in the school would also be happy to answer your questions, so don't hesitate to ask. Things might be second nature to them, but as you're just starting out, it's ok not to know everything. Additionally, check the school website, shared drive, and any policies and procedures, as they often provide answers to your questions. Sometimes, even information that has been sent out to parents can help you find the answer to something.

In summary, be prepared to feel a bit overwhelmed in your first term, but remember you are not alone. Try to enjoy the moment and look for the positives in everyday experiences. Most importantly, take time to relax in the evenings. It is essential to look after yourself and learn to switch off.

First week Checklist

☐ Find out how to do the register

☐ Get a diary/calendar -add dates

☐ Find out about the needs of your class

☐ Read the behaviour policy

☐ Find behaviour strategies to try

☐ Read safeguarding policy

☐ Familiarise yourself with the safeguarding system

Teaching_with_Mrs_Aldridge

Here are the key takeaways for navigating the first term:

1. Overwhelm is normal: It's common to feel overwhelmed in a new job, especially as a teacher. Remember that it's a normal part of the learning process, and things will become more manageable with time and experience.

2. Use the first week checklist: Utilise a checklist to ensure you cover important tasks and get off to a good start in your first week. It can help you stay organised and focused.

3. Take breaks: It's crucial to give yourself breaks and time to recharge. Balancing work and personal life is important for your well-being and effectiveness as a teacher.

4. Preparation is key: Consider preparing meals in advance and getting household chores done on weekends to save time and reduce stress during the week. Being organised in these aspects can free up mental space for your teaching responsibilities.

5. Connect with other teachers: Reach out and talk to other teachers at your school. They are likely experiencing similar challenges and can provide support and guidance. Don't hesitate to ask for help or share your own experiences.

6. Children and LSAs are not intimidating: Remember that children are just children, and LSAs (Learning Support Assistants) are there to support you. Build positive relationships with them and approach interactions with an open and friendly mindset.

7. Believe in yourself: You've worked hard to become a teacher, so have confidence in your abilities. Embrace the journey and try to find joy in the profession. Remember that mistakes and challenges are part of the learning process.

8. Avoid excessive resource purchases: Resist the temptation to buy excessive teaching resources over the summer. Start with the essentials and gradually build up your collection based on your specific needs and teaching style.

9. Ask questions: Don't hesitate to ask questions when you're unsure about something. Seek clarification, guidance, or advice from experienced colleagues or mentors. Asking questions shows your dedication to learning and growing as a teacher.

Keeping these key takeaways in mind, you can navigate your first term more effectively, adapt to the challenges, and focus on providing the best learning experience for your students.

LESSON 2: NURTURING TEACHER WELL-BEING: THE CORNERSTONE OF A THRIVING CLASSROOM

This chapter focuses on an essential part of being a teacher: taking care of your well-being. Teaching can be a challenging job, so it's crucial to prioritise and allocate time for yourself.

My first piece of advice is to determine what suits you best in order to achieve a healthy work-life balance. Consider when it's easier for you to work and when it's more feasible to take time for yourself and your family. This needs to be a priority. For example, some people find it helpful to start their workday early and leave early in the evening to have personal time. Others prefer starting later and working a bit longer after school, allowing them to have time in the morning and after work. Some teachers dedicate a portion of their Sunday afternoon or set aside time on the weekend to reduce their workload during the week. Additionally, some teachers enjoy going for a walk during lunchtime, while others may choose to work through lunch to finish early. Remember, there's no right or wrong answer—there are numerous ways to achieve a good work-life balance. The first step is finding what works for you.

I know a few teacher friends who prefer taking the train to work instead of driving. They utilise this commuting time to catch up on work. Personally, I didn't enjoy travelling long distances to school, so I opted for a job closer to home, which allows me to utilise the free time for activities I love. Some individuals enjoy driving to work, using that time to listen to music or podcasts and enjoying the solitude. Over time, the way you structure your work-life balance may change as other aspects of your life evolve, so be prepared to adapt.

It can be beneficial for some individuals to plan out their week in advance, considering factors such as appointments, workout sessions, and personal activities like reading or cooking. If your schedule changes or unexpected events arise, make sure to find alternative time slots to engage in the activities you enjoy. While it might seem like working more and accomplishing more will make you feel better, in reality, there will always be something more to do. It's important to assess whether a task requires immediate attention or if it can wait until you're at work. A helpful tip is to leave your laptop at work when you plan to have an evening off. By doing so, you eliminate the temptation to work during your personal time.

Teachers often have a multitude of responsibilities, and it can be tempting to work beyond our contracted hours. However, this isn't conducive to your well-being, and it may lead to burnout in the long run. As Early Career Teachers (ECTs), we need to set an example and initiate a change that supports teachers' well-being. It's essential to remember that just because someone else is working extensively doesn't mean you should follow suit. You deserve a break, and sometimes, even your teaching friends need a gentle reminder of that. I've often told my friends that it's okay not to work all the time and emphasised the importance of prioritisation, which I'll delve into further in the next chapter.

You'll likely hear this advice repeatedly, and

you might initially ignore it, but it's crucial not to install school emails or educational programs like Dojo or Seesaw on your phone. Reserve the use of these applications for work time and refrain from bringing them home. While you may believe that you'll have them on your phone just in case and won't check them, trust me, you will, and it's difficult to resist. Maintaining a clear separation between work, phone, and personal life significantly contributes to your well-being.

This brings me to an important point: avoid getting caught up in conversations with parents after your working hours. With the abundance of communication platforms available nowadays, it's tempting to reply to parents immediately. However, consider the time and maintain a professional boundary. Even if you do some work in the evening, it's best to refrain from engaging in parent conversations during that time. Make it clear to parents that you cannot be available 24/7 and establish the school's time limit policy for teacher responses. Parents are generally aware of this policy.

Furthermore, it's perfectly acceptable to say no. This is advice you'll often hear, and initially, you may be inclined to disregard it. However, it's important to embrace this notion. While you should be prepared to be busy as a teacher, it's okay to decline extra responsibilities if you're not given sufficient time to fulfil them. Most schools provide dedicated subject leadership time or ECT time out of the classroom. If this is not the case, don't hesitate to speak up. Teaching is already demanding, and any additional responsibilities should be accompanied by allocated time out of class. If someone asks you to do something after school, but you've already made plans outside of school, it's acceptable to say no unless it's a scheduled staff meeting evening. You can suggest an alternative day when you're available. Remember, you don't have to say yes to everything all the time.

Maintaining a positive mindset is incredibly helpful. It's important to focus on the good aspects of each day. There will always be something that went well, whether it's a successful lesson, accomplishing many tasks on your to-do list, a child surprising you with their learning, or even having a delightful conversation with a student that made you smile. Acknowledge and appreciate the small and big moments that brighten your day. It's easy to become absorbed in the overwhelming workload or stressful situations, but try to let go and embrace the positives.

Another important aspect is sharing your positivity and spreading it throughout the school. In our EYFS team, we always share our little wins from the day, and it's truly heartening to hear about them. Don't hesitate to engage with parents as well, sharing the positive moments with them. In lesson 6, I have dedicated a whole chapter to funny and positive things that children say. These moments brighten my day, and I often share them with others to bring joy into their lives as well.

I will discuss this topic further in the final chapter, but please remember to talk to people. If you've had a challenging day, chances are another teacher has encountered a similar situation, or it might simply be a difficult time of the year for everyone. So, open up about it and communicate with your year group partner or mentor. It's better to express your feelings and concerns, as they may offer valuable advice or help you realise that the situation isn't as bad as you initially thought. Sometimes, taking a step back and looking at the bigger picture reveals that it's not as bad as it seemed.

There is a wealth of advice available online and in other teaching books that provide excellent guidance on teacher well-being. I encourage you to explore these resources if you require further assistance in this area. Most schools have mental health support systems in place, and if you find yourself truly struggling, it would be worthwhile speaking to your GP or a health professional to obtain the appropriate support.

I've had many days when I thought things didn't go well, but when I reflect on all the positive things that happened that day, I begin to realise that what I was worried about was actually quite small. This leads me to my next point: practicing gratitude. It can truly transform a bad day into a good one.

There are various gratitude journals or apps available that people use to write down things they're grateful for at the end of the day. If this works for you, find one that suits your lifestyle. Some people practice gratitude in the morning to set a positive tone for the day, while others do it in the evening to wind down and reflect. Find a method that works best for you. It doesn't have to be complicated. Personally, I don't write anything down, and I don't do it every day. Instead, I simply think about things I'm grateful for when I've had a particularly tough day or need a positive boost.

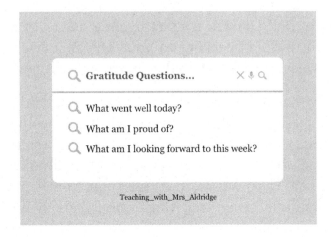

Practicing gratitude is powerful and can help rewire our brains to focus on the positive. It's a simple and quick mood booster, so I highly recommend giving it a try.

It can be particularly challenging in your first few years of teaching to see the good amidst all the new information and overwhelming tasks. However, it's important to give yourself time to reflect on the positives and accept that things don't always go as planned, and that's okay. It happens to all teachers.

The most important part is to recognise when you're feeling overwhelmed and actively seek solutions or ask for advice on how to regain a sense of control.

I know a headteacher and deputy who, when they're having a busy day filled with important decisions and meetings, find solace by visiting classrooms. They engage with the children and staff, discussing positive moments from the day. This is their way of coping and finding uplifting moments. I find their approach inspiring because as teachers, we can get so caught up in our endless to-do lists that we forget to fully enjoy the present and cherish the moments with the children. "Even in the darkest of storms, you will find a rainbow." I genuinely believe that taking a moment to reflect on the progress and goodness in the children can make even the worst day so much better.

In the past six months, I have introduced a weekly reflection activity with my reception class. We have a learning journey display showcasing pictures of our weekly learning, which I update every half term. On Friday afternoons, just before dismissal, we gather around the display and discuss the photos and work from the week. The children share what they enjoyed, and I document their responses, adding them to our working wall. This activity serves as a positive way to end the week and start the weekend.

I have found that incorporating this reflection

practice is not only beneficial for teacher well-being but also for fostering a growth mindset in children. It allows us to reflect on what we have learnt and consider whether we had prior knowledge or if the extra practice helped us achieve something we couldn't do before. We can discuss new skills we have acquired and how we plan to continue using them. Thus, even a brief 5-10 minute chat before dismissal each week can produce valuable insights and contribute to the children's growth and development.

Feel free to adapt this reflection practice to suit your classroom. Whether done verbally or through visual displays, it provides a wonderful opportunity to celebrate achievements and foster a positive learning environment.

Self-care is indeed crucial for teachers, and it's important to prioritise your well-being. Finding a hobby or activity that you enjoy, unrelated to work, is a great way to take care of yourself. Remember to make time for it each week. Additionally, taking care of your physical health by eating well, exercising, and taking breaks is vital. It's easy for these things to slip amidst the busyness of teacher life, but neglecting them can lead to feeling worse over time.

A helpful practice that I carry out which helps my wellbeing is making lists each week. The first list is for meal planning, which helps me stay organised and ensure I'm eating nutritious meals. It also enables me to plan my grocery shopping ahead of time. The second list consists of non-work-related tasks and activities for the week. This can include exercise, rest days, socialising with friends and family, cleaning, gardening, and even self-care activities like taking a bath or reading a book. By incorporating these lists into your routine, you have a better chance of accomplishing tasks and maintaining a balanced life outside of work.

Since implementing these lists, I've experienced a positive shift. I feel more in control, achieve more, and have a sense of accomplishment when I complete my weekly goals. It's important to be kind to yourself and allow flexibility in your plans. If you're exhausted after a long day, it's okay to reschedule some activities for another day. Flexibility and self-awareness are key. Some days, you might exceed your expectations and accomplish even more than you had planned.

Remember, what works for you may be different from what works for others. This book is about sharing your experiences and what has helped you maintain your well-being. It's essential to try different approaches, reflect on their effectiveness, and find a work-life balance that suits your unique lifestyle. Adaptability is crucial, as your circumstances and needs may change over time. However, the constant priority should always be taking care of yourself.

Here are the key takeaways for your looking after your wellbeing:

1. Prioritise self-care: Make your own well-being a priority. Recognise the importance of taking care of yourself physically, mentally, and emotionally.

2. Find your work-life balance: Discover what works best for you in terms of balancing your professional and personal life. Experiment with different strategies until you find a balance that allows you to thrive in both areas.

3. Be adaptable: Life and circumstances can change, so be open to adjusting your routines and strategies accordingly. Flexibility is key in maintaining a healthy work-life balance.

4. Plan and schedule time for yourself: Set aside dedicated time each week for activities and hobbies that bring you joy and relaxation. Use this time to recharge and rejuvenate.

5. Leave work behind: Avoid bringing your work laptop home, if possible, to minimise the temptation of working during your personal time. Create clear boundaries between work and home life.

6. Learn to say no: It's okay to set boundaries and say no when necessary. Don't overcommit yourself and take on more than you can handle. Focus on what truly matters to you and learn to prioritise.

7. Practice positivity and gratitude: Cultivate a positive mindset by focusing on the good things in your life and expressing gratitude. This can help shift your perspective and improve your overall well-being.

8. Seek support and advice: Don't hesitate to reach out to colleagues, friends, or professionals if you need support or advice. Building a strong support

network can provide valuable insights and guidance during challenging times.

By incorporating these key takeaways into your life, you can proactively nurture your well-being and maintain a healthier and more fulfilling work-life balance. Remember, taking care of yourself is essential for long-term success and happiness.

LESSON 3: EMBRACING THE NEVER-END TO-DO LIST

To-do lists can be a really overwhelming part of teaching, so I felt it would be helpful to dedicate a small chapter to this topic. I want to emphasise that feeling overwhelmed by the never-ending list of tasks is completely normal. In this chapter, I aim to provide a few tips that have worked for me in managing my list and prioritising effectively.

During the early stages of my career, I would often come home with a sense of nervousness, wondering how I would ever get through my long to-do list. Despite feeling prepared during the summer, there always seemed to be more tasks to tackle once the school year started. However, it's important to recognise that this is a common experience. The key is learning to prioritise effectively. When considering the tasks on my list, I take the following factors into account:

1. Will it benefit the children?

As teachers, we often come across new ideas or attractive resources on social media that we'd like to try. However, it's crucial to take a closer look and evaluate whether these additions will genuinely benefit the children. Will they offer more advantages compared to the existing resources, which can save you time? It's essential to strike a balance between creating resources and ensuring you are well-rested to be effective in the classroom. Additionally, consider if there is a simpler way to achieve the same impact without sacrificing too much time and energy.

I had a small "oh yeah, that is much easier" moment recently when my colleague and I were about to print out lined paper with a picture for children to practice writing their sentences. Suddenly, we realised that this approach was a complete waste of paper, ink, and time. Instead, why not just have the children use their writing books, which already have lines, and print the photo a couple of times for the tables? They didn't really need their own copy of the picture. It may seem obvious, but when you're busy and caught up in planning and gathering resources, common sense can sometimes escape you. It's totally normal, and we always have a good laugh about it afterward.

2. Do I need it immediately?

There's a tendency to desire a completely clear to-do list. However, some tasks may remain on your list for months. That's okay; they may be things you'll need at some point, but they don't require immediate attention. Prioritise other tasks that are more pressing first.

A popular version of a to-do list that has gained traction is Steven Covey's (2009) four quadrants of time management. While it's used across a range of professions, it's also beneficial for teachers.

On the next page there is an example of how it can be applied to a teacher's to-do list:

FOUR QUADRANTS OF TEACHER TIME MANAGEMENT

1 Urgent & important

Jobs with an impending deadline e.g. resources for lessons that day, setting up the classroom.
Tip - do these immediately.

2 Not Urgent & important

Jobs with a longer deadline e.g. ECT studies, subject leadership jobs, planning for an upcoming meeting. Tip - make a schedule for these jobs.

3 Urgent & not important

E.g. admin jobs, replying to emails, filing, phone calls to do that day, favours for other teachers. Tip - try to delegate some of these jobs.

4 Not Urgent & not important

e.g laminating, labelling, keeping your classroom very tidy, making fancy resources. Tip - eliminate these, there are probably more valuable ways to spend your time.

Teaching_with_Mrs_Aldridge

Sometimes, by the end of the week, I find that if there's something that has been lingering on my to-do list for a long time, it's probably not necessary at all. In those cases, I often decide to completely scrap it. These tasks typically fall into quadrant 4 of Steven Covey's time management matrix—they are neither important nor urgent, so why am I spending time on them? Sometimes, you need to take a step back and reassess to see what truly matters. Time is precious in the teaching profession, so it's important to be mindful of how you allocate it.

3. Is there already a similar resource or program out there that does this?

Before investing hours of your time creating a resource, it's always worth checking if there's something similar already available. With the abundance of websites and teachers sharing resources, you might find that someone has already created what you need, or at least something similar that you can adapt to your specific requirements. Remember the wise old saying, "Don't reinvent the wheel."

In some cases, you can simplify your teaching materials by having one version displayed on the board and having students use their own books or whiteboards to complete the task. This approach can save you from printing out multiple sheets and still achieve the same learning outcomes. It's important to consider whether there's an easier, more efficient way that can also be environmentally friendly.

If you know you'll be teaching the same year group for multiple years, it can be beneficial to laminate certain resources. These laminated materials can cover multiple areas on a single A3 sheet, such as a number line, letter formation reminders, capital letters, full stops, and finger space reminders. We had these on the tables in Year One that the students could access every day, and they can be reused year after year. You can also find pre-made versions of such resources online, so there's no need to worry about creating them yourself. You can find a version in my TES account which you can access at the end of this book. Having a well-organised system to store and manage these laminated resources is also helpful.

4. Do any of my teacher friends already have a similar resource that I can use/borrow?

Absolutely, reaching out to your fellow teachers and asking if they have a similar resource that you can use or borrow is a great idea.

Collaboration and resource sharing among teachers can save a significant amount of time and effort. You may only need a particular resource for a lesson or two, so borrowing it from a colleague who already has it can be a practical solution.

When it comes to planning and creating resources, having year group partners who share the workload equally can be highly beneficial. By coordinating with your colleagues, you can avoid duplicating efforts and distribute the resources efficiently. For example, if you're making a resource, you can create two copies and give one to the other class. Additionally, taking turns planning different subjects each term can ensure a fair division of responsibilities. If you teach lessons on different days, you can share the same resources, eliminating the need to create duplicates for a limited number of uses. These strategies promote teamwork and help reduce the length of your to-do lists.

To efficiently tackle your to-do list during your PPA (Planning, Preparation, and Assessment) or ECT (Early Career Teacher) time, it can be beneficial to start with the quickest tasks first. This approach allows you to see immediate progress as you check off those smaller items, which can boost your motivation to continue completing other tasks. The same principle applies when you're at home—beginning with smaller jobs creates a sense of accomplishment, encouraging you to keep going and tackle larger tasks.

Using your lunch break strategically is another effective way to manage your workload. Allocating half an hour to eat and chat with colleagues while using the remaining half-hour to complete tasks can help prevent feeling overwhelmed during your PPA time or after school. It's a valuable opportunity to make progress on your to-do list without sacrificing personal time outside of work.

It is absolutely correct that teaching often involves juggling multiple tasks and being prepared for various changes. It's important to find effective strategies for staying organised and keeping track of everything.

Using a diary to write down school events and meetings is a great approach to staying organised. By documenting these important dates, you can ensure that you don't miss any crucial events or appointments. Opting for an erasable pen allows for flexibility in case there are any changes or adjustments to the schedule.

It helps maintain a clean and organised diary without having to cross out or scribble over outdated information.

Similarly, using post-it notes on your laptop screen for your to-do list is a practical solution. It keeps your list easily accessible, especially since you have your laptop with you most of the time. The advantage of digital notes is that they can be easily modified, removed, or rearranged without leaving a cluttered or crossed-out mess. The availability of different colours and sizes allows you to categorise tasks based on different areas, such as SEND, subject leadership, classroom jobs, and PPA. This method provides a visual reminder of your tasks without the risk of misplacing or losing your notes.

However, it's important to note that different individuals have different preferences, and some may prefer traditional paper-based systems. The key is to find what works best for you and your organisational style.

Remember, managing your to-do list is about finding a balance and not allowing it to overwhelm you. Implementing the tips and advice you've learnt can help you streamline your tasks and reduce the length of your list. It's also important to recognise that there will always be items on your to-do list, and that's okay. Take it one task at a time, prioritise effectively, and celebrate each accomplishment as you move forward.

Here are the key takeaways for organising and prioritising your to do list:

1. Consider the value: Before adding a task to your list, ask yourself if it will truly benefit the children. Assess the impact and prioritise accordingly.

2. Urgency assessment: Determine if the task requires immediate attention or if it can be deferred. Not all items on your list need to be addressed right away.

3. Resource availability: Check if there are existing resources or programs that can fulfil the same purpose. Avoid reinventing the wheel and utilise what's already available.

4. Collaborate with colleagues: Reach out to your teacher friends and colleagues to see if they have similar resources or materials that you can use or borrow. Sharing responsibilities can save time and effort.

5. Four quadrants of time management: Utilise the four quadrants approach (urgency vs. importance) to categorise your tasks and prioritise them effectively.

6. Maintain a diary: Add important dates, events, and meetings to your diary. Consider using an erasable pen to accommodate any changes or updates.

7. Share tasks with colleagues: Collaborate with your colleagues to distribute tasks and responsibilities, preventing duplication of efforts.

8. Electronic to-do lists: Consider using electronic tools such as digital notes or apps to manage your to-do list efficiently. This allows for easy modification and accessibility.

9. Start with small or urgent tasks: Begin with quick and manageable tasks to make progress and build momentum. Addressing smaller tasks first can help create a sense of accomplishment.

10. Take control and avoid overwhelm: Remember that you are in control of your to-do list. Take steps to manage it

effectively and prevent it from becoming overwhelming.

By incorporating these strategies, you can better organise, prioritise, and manage your to-do list, leading to increased productivity and a more balanced workload.

LESSON 4: MASTERING TRANSITIONS: NAVIGATING THE EXHAUSTING YET PRICELESS JOURNEY

There are numerous transitions that take place throughout a classroom every day, and how you execute them can truly make a difference in both your and the children's experience. It's important to consider how transitions will look in your classroom and find effective strategies that work for you and your class. I've discovered that this may vary each year depending on the group of children. Transitions can sometimes feel a bit chaotic with children moving around, but they are a significant part of a teacher's day. In this chapter, I want to share some of my experiences with transitions and the strategies I've employed.

During my first year of teaching, my year one class excelled at transitions. They enjoyed trying out new things, so I would experiment with different attention-getters and ways of lining up. However, my next class preferred familiarity. If I said something one day and not the next, they would ask why I didn't say it. They thrived on having the same routine, and it worked well for them, which was perfectly fine.

Most children and adults appreciate routines, so keeping transitions similar and providing ample notice when something is changing is beneficial. For instance, most days, you'll change lessons at a similar time, and your routines for breaks, lunch, and the end of the day will be fairly consistent. However, if there's a school event or a change to the normal routine such as a school trip, it's important to inform the children in advance and explain the reason for the change.

Visual timetables are effective tools for informing children about what's happening. There are various ways to create visual timetables, such as using printed and laminated pictures that you add to a timetable on your wall. Alternatively, some teachers opt for virtual timetables that can be displayed on a screen. If you use Google Classroom frequently, especially with KS2 children, you can add the timetable to the classroom for easy access. Visual timetables not only reduce anxiety related to unknown events but also provide support for children with special educational needs and disabilities (SEND). They can also help you stay on track, particularly when there are changes to the schedule.

Lining up is a common transition in schools. Some teachers allow children to line up in a random order, while others prefer a specific order. In my first year, my class managed well with a random order. I established a few rules regarding certain children who shouldn't stand next to each other in line (as they tended to get carried away), and I usually chose my line leader or end of the line wisely. This approach worked effectively, so I didn't need to spend excessive time teaching them a particular order or creating an order that worked.

However, in my next class at a different school, the kitchen staff preferred the children to line up in alphabetical order for more efficient lunchtime organisation. This was perfectly fine, and during the first week (particularly in Early Years), we practiced the order numerous times. To facilitate this, each child made a painting of themselves as part of our "All About Me" topic. I hung these paintings in order from the ceiling, allowing the children to visually see their position in the line. The only challenge arose when we needed to separate certain children during lunchtime, which required adjusting the order. However, since only a couple of children changed spaces, the other staff members quickly learnt their new positions.

Transitioning from the carpet or tables to the line is another mission in itself. I primarily work in Early Years and Year 1, so this process might be easier for older children—I'm not sure. Nevertheless, it doesn't hurt to explore different strategies, which can also make the transition a bit of fun and an opportunity to practice various skills, even for older children. Here are a few ideas for getting your class to line up:

1. Phonics Practise: In Early Years and Year 1, I like to use phonics as a way to line up. I might say a sound, and if a child's name contains that sound, they can line up. In Early Years, I initially start with the letter their name starts with and gradually progress to the whole first and last names if they know the spelling. You could also adapt this approach by using the names of the alphabet, allowing them to practice letter recognition. Writing the sound or letter (lowercase or capital) on the board and having children line up if it's in their

name is a great way to reinforce visual recognition as well.

2. "Simon Says" or "Mrs/Mr/Miss [Teacher's Name] Says": This classic game is always a hit in my class. I give instructions like "Mrs. Aldridge says line up if you have brown hair" or "Mrs. Aldridge says line up if you are wearing a jumper." It's not only great for vocabulary practice but also helpful for English as an Additional Language (EAL) children. I also like to add in a few trick instructions to test their listening skills.

3. Singing: Who doesn't love a song? You could have a designated song that the children sing while lining up. There are online resources with songs specifically created for lining up that you could use. Alternatively, you could play an upbeat song to encourage the children to move quickly to the line.

4. Play a Game: Incorporate a game into the transition by asking the children to walk like a specific animal, such as a penguin or a giant, or march like a soldier. I usually send a row or table at a time. If they're talking, I always remind them that animals don't talk. It's a fun way to manage the classroom.

5. Retrieval Practise: Use lining up as an opportunity for retrieval practice. You

can ask for number bonds to 5 or 10, or a fact about something you've taught them. Once they provide the correct answer, they can line up. If you have some children who may not want to answer in front of others, you can save their turn for the end so they only have to tell you. If whiteboards and pens are readily available, they can write the answer on the whiteboard and put it away on their way to the line.

6. Random Name Generator: For a fun and effective way to promote name recognition in Early Years, try using a random name generator. Simply input all of the children's names into the generator, spin it, and whoever it lands on has to line up. This method adds an element of excitement and encourages children to practice identifying and reading their own name. I found it to be a helpful strategy last year as it provided a truly random way of organising the line.

So, in my experience, transitions can sometimes become an opportunity for children to engage in random conversations, especially in my second class. Picture this: you have a class of 25 4-5-year-olds, it's lunchtime, and everyone is hungry. You've already gone through the transition of washing hands and collecting coats, and now you need to transition to the line for a walk to the hall. You come up with an effective way to send a few children at a time to line up, but out of the 25, 19 line up beautifully, while the remaining 6 surround you, eager to share something random. One child wants to talk about their pet snakes, another one suddenly remembers they forgot to wash their hands, someone needs to use the toilet right at that moment, someone wants to inform you that their dad's birthday is next Thursday, another child compliments your glasses (the same ones you wear every day), and the final child realises they mistakenly told you this morning that they were having a packed lunch when they actually don't.

To address this challenge, I've learnt to provide them with 5 minutes before lunch to talk to me, their Learning Support Assistant (LSA), or their friends, allowing them to get it out of their system before we line up. I also encourage them to engage in conversations with each other and us during continuous provision time. They love sharing stories about their weekends or their pets, so it's nice to provide an appropriate time for these interactions.

Another significant transition occurs when moving to or from the carpet. It could be from working at the tables or after tidying up from continuous provision, or even when coming in from break times. Here are a few strategies I use with my class:

One of their absolute favourite strategies (although I use it sparingly to maintain its effectiveness) is when I turn around to face the board and inform them that I need them to be seated in their carpet spot, ready to learn, before I turn back around. My LSA is there to keep an eye on them and discreetly signal me when I can turn around. I have never seen them move so quickly—it's great!

Another strategy I love is either counting up or down from 20. They need to be seated by the time I reach either 20 or 0. This not only helps them practice their counting skills but also allows me to monitor and support any students who may be distracted along the way as we count together.

We also have a carpet song to the tune of Frère Jacques, which is fantastic because the children love singing it. They are seated before it ends, and we can cover some basic rules in the song.

It goes like this:

Find your spot,

Find your spot,

And sit down,

And sit down,

We are looking,

We are listening,

We are ready,

3, 2, 1

I might do something similar to the above, but with some mindful breathing exercises. I will be at the front and start doing some mindful breathing, finger breathing, rainbow breaths, etc., and the children have to join in. I find it especially effective after a break time or lunchtime. Alternatively, I could start a mindfulness video as they are coming in, and they are expected to sit down and join in. We sometimes watch videos of lava moving around, ocean animals swimming, or engage in some yoga exercises.

Another strategy I use is simply putting a timer on. After lunch, the children usually get their water bottles and come to the carpet for the register. I might then set a 1-minute timer to give them enough time to collect their bottles and sit down before it ends.

There's a good strategy using numbers. I might say, "Number 1 is to put down what you are doing, number 2 is to walk to the carpet, and number 3 is to sit down." The students can only perform those actions when I show the corresponding number of fingers. This strategy eliminates the need for verbal instructions and allows me to observe who is paying attention and following the instructions. You can use this strategy in various ways throughout the day, and I find that three sets of instructions work well.

Sometimes, I might ask them to come to the carpet and copy my actions. I will sit at the front and tap my head, clap my hands, tap my knees, rub my belly, etc., and then they all join in. Once everyone has joined in, I begin the lesson. This activity is also great for ensuring that you have the students' attention before starting the lesson. There are other attention getters you can try out, and you can find more ideas online or ask teacher friends for suggestions.

Here are a few ideas:

- You can simply count down from 10 or 5 and let the students know that you expect them to be ready to learn by the time you reach 0. As you count down, you can say phrases like "Ready to learn in 5," "Super sitting in 4," "Looking this way in 3," "Not talking in 2," "Learning hats on in 1," and finally "0." This way, you can remind them of some important rules while getting their attention and preparing them for the upcoming lesson.

- There are numerous call and response ideas that teachers can use to engage students. For example, you can say "Are we ready?" and the students would respond with "Yes, we are!" Another option is saying "Macaroni cheese" and having the students reply with "Everyone freeze." It's beneficial to have a repertoire of different call and response phrases to keep the classroom dynamic and interactive.

- Using a small bell as a signal is a great strategy to get students' attention. When you ring the bell, the children stop what they are doing, look at you, and listen. Additionally, having them wave their fingers in the air or place their hands on their heads while you're speaking can help ensure that they are fully engaged and not distracted by objects they may be holding. These visual cues can be effective in redirecting their focus and promoting active listening during specific moments of instruction.

- Having a recognition board in your classroom is a wonderful way to acknowledge and reinforce positive behaviours. By verbally recognising specific children who are demonstrating readiness to learn or exemplary behaviour, you are providing positive reinforcement and setting an example for the rest of the class. This can motivate other students to follow suit in order to receive recognition as well. Adding the child's photo to the physical board further emphasises their achievement and serves as a visual reminder of their positive behaviour. It's a great way to create a positive classroom culture and encourage students to strive for excellence.

Giving children a time warning before transitioning from one activity to another is indeed a valuable practice. Providing a 5-minute warning allows them to mentally prepare for the upcoming change and helps minimise any feelings of sudden disruption or anxiety. This is particularly beneficial for children with special educational needs (SEND), as it gives them additional time to process the transition and adjust accordingly.

By incorporating time warnings into your routine, you are promoting a sense of predictability and structure within the classroom. Children become more aware of the passing time and can better manage their tasks and emotions accordingly. It also encourages a smoother transition as they can wrap up their current activities or tasks before moving on.

Remembering to give time warnings becomes easier with practice and can become a natural part of your teaching approach. The benefits extend beyond children with SEND and can positively impact the overall classroom environment, fostering a sense of respect, understanding, and cooperation among students.

Transition days are indeed significant events in a school year, and as a teacher, it's crucial to be mindful of the emotions and challenges that students may face during this time. Moving up to a new year group and transitioning to a new teacher can evoke feelings of excitement, anticipation, and anxiety for many children. It's essential to create a supportive and nurturing environment to help them navigate these changes successfully.

Recognising the range of emotions children may experience during transition days is important. Some may feel nervous about the unknowns and adjustments they'll have to make, while others may have mixed feelings about leaving their current teacher, classmates, and routines behind. Acknowledging and validating these emotions can go a long way in helping children feel understood and supported during this transitional period.

End-of-year tiredness can also add an additional layer of challenge to transition days. It's important to balance the excitement of the upcoming changes with the need for rest and self-care. Providing opportunities for relaxation, reflection, and open discussions about their experiences and concerns can help alleviate some of the exhaustion and foster a sense of emotional well-being.

For children who experience frequent transitions, such as those from military families or students moving between schools, the impact can be particularly significant. Creating a strong support network within the school and offering additional resources, such as transition programs or peer support, can help ease the challenges they face and provide a sense of stability and belonging.

When welcoming new students or saying goodbye to those leaving the school, it's vital to consider the impact on their well-being. Providing a warm and inclusive environment for new students helps them adjust more easily, while bidding farewell to departing students with meaningful goodbyes can help them leave with positive memories and a sense of closure.

By prioritising the emotional well-being of students during transition days and offering support throughout the process, teachers can help them navigate these changes more smoothly and promote a positive learning environment for all.

Transition days can vary greatly between schools and year groups. It's essential to familiarise yourself with the specific approach and schedule adopted by your school, especially if you're new to the school. Collaborating with your new year group partner can also be beneficial in planning and preparing for the transition day.

For early years, stay and play sessions are commonly used to introduce new intake children to the school environment. These sessions allow smaller groups of children to visit the school and become familiar with the surroundings and routines. Depending on the school, these sessions may take place before the summer or in September. If you're an early years teacher, it's also advantageous to enquire about participating in visits to nurseries, as this can help establish relationships with future pupils.

If you're transitioning to a new school in the summer, it's important to communicate with your current headteacher and request time off for the transition day at your new school. Many schools recognise the significance of these days and are supportive in facilitating your attendance. Additionally, they may arrange for a substitute teacher to cover your class during your absence.

Transition days and stay and play sessions play a vital role in reducing anxiety and facilitating a smooth transition for both students and parents. It provides an opportunity for pupils to ask questions, become familiar with their new teacher, and start building relationships. The supportive and welcoming environment created during these sessions can help alleviate concerns and create a positive foundation for the upcoming school year.

Transitions are indeed a significant aspect of teaching, and it's important to plan and implement various strategies throughout the year. Starting strong with a few confident strategies in the first week is crucial, but don't be afraid to experiment and try different approaches as the year progresses. Adapting to the needs and dynamics of your class will contribute to a successful and engaging learning environment.

Here are the key takeaways for navigating transitions:

1. Find some attention getting strategies you will use.

2. Decide which strategy to use to get your class to line up.

3. Use a visual timetable and time warnings so children are aware that a transition is impending.

4. Plan for transition day.

5. Consider the impact on staff and pupils wellbeing and offer support where needed.

LESSON 5: THE TWO-YEAR ECT FRAMEWORK: MY PERSPECTIVES AND INSIGHTS

My main reason for writing this book was because I was in the first cohort of the new ECT framework, which involved a two-year induction period. I thought it might be helpful for some people if I shed a bit of light on what this involves. Then, I wanted to add some extra chapters to share my experiences and offer some advice.

The new framework is very sensitive to workload. As we all know, teachers are super busy, and they have really taken this into account with the new framework. There are small bite-sized pieces of learning for each week or two weeks, depending on which year you are in, and these are completely manageable within your ECT time out of class.

Your school will be attached to a provider that is running the course, and your school will provide you with a mentor. If you move schools during your induction year, it doesn't matter because you can just transfer to the provider at your new school. I moved schools between year one and year two, and it was very straightforward moving across. I just needed a bit of time to get used to the new platform, but everyone at my provider was helpful, and I had another ECT in my school who gave me some advice as she had used it in year one.

Your provider will give you an overview of the two years. It will probably involve:

- Weekly mentor meetings
- Some face to face training
- Online training/ conferences
- Self-study materials
- Observations of your teaching
- Observing other teachers

Your mentor will conduct a lesson dip, typically lasting about 15-20 minutes, every week in your first year and every other week in your second year. These lesson dips are incredibly valuable and supportive. Your mentor will discuss the positive aspects of your lesson and may provide you with advice or ideas to further enhance your teaching practice. Having an approachable mentor is key, as you can freely ask them any questions you may have.

In addition to the lesson dips, you will also have regular mentor meetings, typically on a weekly or bi-weekly basis in the second year. These meetings provide a dedicated space to discuss your lessons, address any concerns, and explore other professional development opportunities. It's during these meetings that you can engage in instructional coaching sessions, where you have the chance to practice implementing new strategies and receive feedback.

The two-year timeframe of the ECT framework allows for ample support and guidance. Take advantage of this time by actively seeking help and asking questions. Your mentors are there to assist you and provide the necessary support for your growth as a teacher.

It's important to acknowledge that personal experiences with mentors may vary, and some individuals may have different levels of satisfaction with their mentorship. If you find that your relationship with your mentor is not as supportive as you would like, rest assured that there are alternative options in place to ensure you receive the necessary support. Don't hesitate to explore these alternatives if needed.

It's worth mentioning that my positive experiences with my mentors during my training year and first two years have shaped my perception of the new framework. I am aware that not everyone may have had the same experience, but I believe that the support and guidance provided during the two-year induction period are crucial for the professional development of early career teachers.

The timing of online conferences can vary between providers. In my second year, the conferences were held during the school day, typically from 14:00 to 15:30. However, in my first year, the provider scheduled them after school from 16:00 to 17:30. Personally, I preferred the conferences during the school day as it allowed me to have the evening free to prepare my classroom for the following day. Your school will release you to attend these conferences during the school day, recognising their importance in your professional development.

The framework also includes both in-person

and online training sessions with other ECTs. These sessions provide a valuable opportunity to share experiences and practice teaching strategies. However, I noticed that it would have been more beneficial if the pairing of ECTs took into account the age group they were teaching. At times, I was paired up with secondary teachers, and although some experiences overlapped, I found that speaking with other EYFS and KS1 teachers was more relevant and advantageous. Feedback from other ECTs regarding the program has echoed this concern. I am hopeful that this feedback will be taken into consideration for the next cohort, with a focus on pairing ECTs who teach similar age groups for more meaningful exchanges.

Through my experience with the two-year ECT framework, I found that the amount of self-study required was manageable and aligned with the extra time allocated for ECTs. In the first year, with an additional 10% off-timetable, there is more self-study involved. However, I felt that the workload was still manageable during this time. In the second year, with a 5% reduced timetable, I found the workload to be well-balanced within the allocated ECT time. It's important to stay focused during your ECT time and prioritise training and acquiring new information, even though it can be tempting to get side-tracked with other tasks.

The self-study materials provided as part of the framework include a combination of reading materials, case studies, videos showcasing teaching examples, and quizzes. I appreciated the variety of formats as it helped me stay engaged and motivated. Additionally, there are often stretch modules available for those who wish to delve deeper into specific topics.

I highly recommend making time to observe other teachers, as it is an invaluable learning opportunity. This is what your ECT release time is intended for. By observing other teachers, you can gather great ideas for behaviour management strategies and lesson planning. It's not necessary to spend your entire ECT time solely on observations; instead, try to strike a balance between observations and engaging with the self-study materials. In every school I've worked in, teachers have been willing to allow me to observe their classes, so make sure to take advantage of this opportunity and observe a variety of teachers across different year groups and lessons.

For me, the two-year induction period has been an excellent experience. I have learnt a lot and had the chance to practice new ideas. I feel prepared to continue my teaching journey, and I'm aware that other teachers are always ready to share advice and offer support. I also feel that I am now in a position to provide support to others, which is why I wanted to write this book. My goal is to share my experiences, offer support, and let you know that what you're feeling is completely normal. The past two years have flown by quickly, and I'm grateful for the extended timeframe of the induction period. I believe that one year would have been too short. Additionally, I have found it helpful to switch year groups during this time, as it allowed me to experience both EYFS and year one while benefiting from the additional support of my mentors.

While there are ample opportunities to discuss training-related experiences, I've noticed that there is limited opportunity to share our general thoughts and feelings about teaching. In my first year, I was the only ECT in my school, and although my mentor was fantastic and had been through the early years of teaching herself, I found it valuable to connect with other teachers who were also starting their careers. In my current school, there are two of us in our second year and two first-year ECTs, and it's been wonderful to have the chance to chat with them. Never underestimate the importance of talking to others. Throughout this book, you'll notice my emphasis on the value of communication, as it greatly contributes to my overall well-being. Having the opportunity to realise that others share similar experiences and feelings is incredibly important.

This chapter offers a subjective perspective based on my personal experience with specific schools and ECT providers. It's important to note that the details may vary depending on your specific provider. I encourage you to refer to the official framework (DfE 2019), and gather more information about your particular provider's induction period, as they will provide you with comprehensive details on how their program operates.

While navigating through the two-year ECT framework, I encourage you to embrace the process and make the most of this unique experience. These two years are invaluable, and you won't have the opportunity to relive them. Be open to receiving advice, exploring new activities, and trying out different approaches in your classroom. Learn from other teachers and draw inspiration from their practices. Most importantly, find joy in being with your students and strive to find positives in every day. Enjoy this journey of growth and discovery.

Here are the key takeaways for your two-year ECT induction:

1. Familiarise yourself with the information provided by your ECT provider.

2. Refer to the framework to understand your entitlements and expectations.

3. Allocate time for observing other teachers and gaining ideas and inspiration.

4. Don't hesitate to ask questions and seek support from your mentors and colleagues.

5. Embrace the journey and find joy in the learning and growth opportunities it offers.

Remember, this is an exciting period of professional development, so make the most of it and enjoy the process of becoming an experienced and confident teacher.

LESSON 6: UNLEASHING THE LAUGHTER: CHILDREN'S HILARIOUS REMARKS

Honestly, the children are the best part about being a teacher. I could easily fill multiple chapters with their stories, but I have selected my favourite moments and quotes from my first two years of teaching. In my first year, I taught Year One, and in my second year, I taught Reception, so I've had my fair share of experiences with 4-6-year-olds.

The girl who couldn't be tricked
During our animal-themed topic in my first year, we used an AI app to engage the children. We pretended that some animals had escaped from the zoo and made a mess in our classroom. We even placed footprints on the floor and claimed to have caught it on CCTV. Most

children were amazed and excited by this, but there was one child who remained unconvinced. Confidently, she explained that we had simply put flour on the floor and created footprints by drawing holes in it. I felt a tinge of sadness that she missed out on the innocence of it all, but it was amusing that she couldn't be tricked.

Now, let's talk about the nativity play - a lovely yet challenging time of year for any Reception or KS1 teacher. Contrary to popular films, we are not all like Mr. Poppy! During a dress rehearsal, while waiting for the Shepherds to enter the stage, three out of four Shepherds made their appearance. The other reception teacher and I exchanged glances, hoping the remaining Shepherd would realise and join them. Instead, he looked at us and said, "What are you two looking at?" At that point, we couldn't help but burst into laughter.

One more nativity moment to share In my class, one of the children had the role of the narrator. She knew she would be reading parts of the script along with a few other children. A few days later, her Mum approached my LSA (Learning Support Assistant) and said that her child didn't want to be a "radiator" in the play. My LSA did an excellent job of keeping a straight face and explained that her role was, in fact, that of the narrator. We went over the part again and described the costume to the child. Fast forward five months, and I was reading a story to the class. I asked them what we call the person who writes the story. The same child raised her hand and confidently declared, "radiator." We had another conversation to clarify the meaning of "narrator," and thankfully, another child knew the answer to my original question—a writer is called an author. Since then, I haven't looked at a radiator the same way.

The most polite refusal
As most of you know, teachers try to listen to each child read their reading book every week. In my second year, due to being in Reception, this happened during continuous provision. There was a particular child in my class who loved being creative in the building area and could focus on something for a long time. However, it was his turn for reading, so I asked him as I always had since September, "It's your turn for reading. Can you get your books, please?" Usually, the children would go straight away and get their books, as they loved the one-on-one time. But on this day, his response was, "No, thank you." His answer was so sure and confident, and it caught myself and my LSA off guard, making us burst into laughter. I had to

talk to him about the expectations, and he eventually went and got his reading book.

Parents consultation evening

In my second year, I had a child in my class who was known for his brilliant one-liners. During our parent-teacher evenings, the children were invited to attend, allowing us to discuss their positive learning experiences, progress, and areas that might need improvement. On one occasion, some parents asked if there was anything they could work on at home to help their son. I suggested practicing handwriting, as he found some letters tricky to form. The child responded with a confident "No, I don't." We all burst out laughing, and his parents were a little embarrassed. After talking to the child about the specific letters he found challenging, he agreed to practice at home.

More parents consultation fun

In my EYFS class, I had a cheeky and talkative boy who loved sharing stories about his family and their adventures during holidays and weekends. During a parent-teacher evening, his mum and dad accompanied him. As I discussed his progress, the child chimed in, saying, "My dad sneaks into the kitchen at night-time and has snacks, but I'm not allowed, and I find all of his mess in the morning." Although it was a funny comment, his mum confirmed that, indeed, his dad enjoyed a midnight snack. A few moments later, the child added, "And my dad swears all the time!" At this point, his dad turned bright red, and after explaining to the child that some adults do swear but he shouldn't, we redirected the conversation back to discussing the child's progress and not his dad.

That's why you need to strike During recent teacher strikes, our school was completely closed for a few days. We had discussed the strikes with the children, and their parents had done the same. The day after one of the strike days, I had a conversation with a child in my class:

Child A: "I forgot to pay for my snack Mrs Aldridge." (we use pennies to pay for their snack to practise counting and money skills)

Me: "Don't worry, you can go and pay now."

Child A: "Ok, there's a lot of fruit, it looks like you have a snack shop."

Me: "Maybe I should start selling it properly and make some money like a real shop."

Child A: "Then you wouldn't need to strike."

I couldn't believe this comment came from a 4-year-old! It was a funny moment, and I ended up sharing the story with other staff members throughout the day, brightening their day as well.

Are we too loud?
On a day when I went home at lunchtime due to a migraine, I didn't get a chance to talk to my class as it came on suddenly. One of the LSAs covered my class and let them know that I had gone home because I had a headache. One of the children responded, "Is that because we are so loud?"

Laying an egg
To set the scene for this one, our topic was 'Ready Steady, Grow,' and we were learning about plants and animals growing. On a particular day, each child made a picture of the life cycle of a hen. This 4-year-old child had a 25-minute car journey home, so her mum reminded her to go to the toilet before leaving school. When she returned from the toilet, she

said, "Mrs. Aldridge, when I went to the toilet, I sat like a hen laying an egg." I found this link between our learning and her statement hilarious. Her mum was slightly confused until I explained what we had learnt earlier that day!

A tray full of stones

This next story warms my heart more than it makes me laugh, but I feel it's worth sharing. In our outdoor area, we have a stone pit for digging and transporting tiny stones. I kept finding random stones in the classroom for a few weeks and wondered how they were getting inside. One day, as I was putting letters in the children's trays to go home, I discovered a big stash of stones inside one of the boys' trays. I showed him that I had found them, and he said, "I wanted to put them in my garden because we don't have many stones at home." I thought it was a very caring gesture.

Sharing our Geography learning

In the summer term with my Early Years class, the Geography lead wanted to do a pupil voice session with children from each year group. We selected one child from each class who we thought would be confident enough to speak about our bears unit, which had a geography focus, and tell her about the different habitats and countries we had learnt about. As part of our curriculum, we also went to the forest every week, which had many connections to geography. On the way to meet the Geography lead, a child in my class asked, "What is geography?" This wasn't unusual for Early Years, as for us, it is called "Understanding the World," but it was still a slightly cringe-worthy moment.

After the pupil voice session, we asked the Geography lead how it went. She was laughing to herself before informing us that the child in my class kept telling her off for talking to the other child more. We knew that assertiveness was part of her character, and we had reminded her to be patient, but it's challenging when she's interacting with a child she doesn't know. Thankfully, the Geography lead found it quite amusing.

A great maps lesson
But that wasn't the end of it. The other child told the Geography lead about using maps in the forest to find squirrels, describing the whole activity of following a route on the map. The Geography lead asked her if the map was helpful, and she confidently replied, "Yes, we found the squirrels." At this point, the child in my class started insisting that we didn't do this activity. Given her assertiveness earlier, the

Geography lead didn't believe her. She then asked myself and the other EYFS teacher about when we did this lovely activity. We burst out laughing and couldn't stop as we told her that we hadn't done it. The child had fabricated this impressive activity, which had impressed the Geography lead, but it wasn't true at all. We had planned to use maps in the forest the following half-term, but we hadn't implemented the activity yet.

Between those two children, the pupil voice session didn't go quite as expected, but it certainly brightened our day on the last day of the half-term.

Appreciate the good days
In our staff room, we have a board where we can add post-it notes about funny things children have said. I really enjoy having this in the staff room as it can brighten your day and someone else's. I have been making notes for my book over the last two years, and writing this chapter has reminded me of all the funny times. So, if there's anything you can take away from this chapter, it's to make a note of all the funny things. Maybe suggest that your school sets up a similar board in the staff room. You'll appreciate the chance to look back and remember the joyous moments.

Here are the key takeaways for children say the funniest things:

1. Try to enjoy your time with the children. Don't take everything too seriously.

2. Laugh and smile with your class.

3. Appreciate the lovely, unique characteristics of children.

4. Share the joy and share these moments with other people, teachers, your family/friends and parents of your class.

LESSON 7: FROM APPLICATION TO EDUCATOR: UNRAVELLING THE JOB APPLICATION PROCESS

As most of the readers of my book will be trainee teachers ready to embark on their teaching journey, I thought it would be helpful to discuss the job process. With three successful teaching jobs in three years, I have experienced various interview processes, and I am willing to share both my successes and failures. I want to start by emphasising that you should never give up. The process can be tough and emotionally draining, but you will find a position that is right for you.

As you approach the end of your trainee year, you will begin the job-hunting process. It can become quite intense, juggling training tasks, placements, and searching for a job. However, remember that this feeling won't last forever, and many others are in the same position as you. Reach out to other trainees to share experiences, talk to your mentor, colleagues at your training provider, or the teachers you are working with. There are plenty of people available to offer advice. In my experience, the training provider offered talks on the job process and mock interviews for those who wanted to practice. Take advantage of these valuable opportunities if you feel anxious or unsure.

Firstly, before you start your search, consider drafting your personal statement. There are numerous examples available online. Having a first draft ready beforehand will alleviate some pressure. Once you find a job you want to apply for, you can tailor your statement to match the criteria and values of the school. Seek feedback from family, friends, colleagues, or your training provider to refine your statement.

Next, subscribe to your local job advert service to receive notifications for new job openings. Some positions may explicitly state that they are open to Early Career Teachers (ECTs), while others may not. It's worth enquiring. Finding the right school is crucial as each one has its own unique environment. Additionally, always make it a point to tour the schools this will enable you to learn more about the school's operations, teacher workload, curriculum, ECT support, and get to know the staff you will interact with. This is also an opportunity for you to showcase your personality. Approach the visit with confidence, armed with questions about aspects you want to explore. Take note of everything you observe, compliment displays or work that impresses you, and look for things that ignite your interest and make you want to work there (these are the elements you'll want to highlight in your personal statement).

On the next page is a list of general questions I typically ask, but feel free to adapt them based on the year group you are interested in:

SCHOOL TOUR QUESTIONS

Can you tell me about your curriculum?

What support will be in place for an ECT?

Which phonics scheme do you use? How does this work?

How do you promote reading for pleasure here?

How do you allocate PPA time and support staff?

Do you follow any other schemes?

How do you support staff and pupil wellbeing?

What is your approach to behaviour management?

How would you describe the feel of the school?

What is the vision for the school?

Teaching_with_Mrs_Aldridge

After the tour, it's important to reflect and decide whether you want to apply for the position or not. Don't feel pressured to apply for every job you come across. It's okay to not apply if you didn't get a good sense of the school or if your values don't align. Consider your own well-being and happiness working there. For example, I toured a school where the head teacher emphasized the long hours and intense workload expected from teachers. This level of intensity felt overwhelming even before applying for the position. Remember, you know your own work style and the type of people you work well with, so ensure the school feels right for you.

The next step is to apply for the position, adjusting your personal statement to reflect what you liked and learnt during the school tour. It's perfectly fine to explore multiple schools and apply for those that interest you. Keep in mind that not every application will result in an interview, as the competition can be fierce. If you'd like to understand why you weren't selected, consider asking for feedback on your application, which can be helpful for future job applications.

When I was searching for my first job, I noticed many familiar faces from my training provider during school tours. Initially, this made me nervous, but it's important to remember that we are all in the same boat, and there is a job out there that suits everyone. It's also possible to love a school during the tour but realise it's not the right fit once you start working there. That's why I eventually moved from my first school. My values didn't align with the academies, and the changes happening at the school during my first year didn't match the way I wanted to teach.

After submitting your application, you will wait to hear if you have been selected for an interview. The interview process can vary but generally involves a formal interview and teaching a lesson. Some schools might also ask you to take a SATs test, have lunch with the children, or answer questions from students.

Once you receive this information, if the school hasn't provided much information about the class, I recommend sending an email to request additional details. In the resources section, you can find a link to my TES where you can access a draft email that you can use. I typically ask:

1. How many pupils are in the class? (so, you can make sure you have enough resources)

2. Are there any SEND or SEMH needs that you need to know about? This way you can make some adaptations to support the pupils.

3. Will there be an LSA in the classroom to support the pupils? (think about what you want them to do, write it on the plan)

4. Will you have access to an interactive whiteboard if you need one? Also find out how you can connect to this, in case you need to email your presentation across or get a USB stick.

5. Finally, think about what resources you will need and ask the school if they can get these prepared for your lesson. There is nothing worse than assuming they have something your placement school has and turning up to find out they don't have it.

Hopefully, you have experience from your training years that will help you plan your lesson observation. If you have taught a lesson during the year that went well and meets the criteria, consider teaching that lesson. It's important to feel comfortable and confident in what you are teaching. You can always ask your mentor for advice on your lesson plan or try it out with your placement class. Since you don't know the children, it can be challenging, so ensure you are completely confident with the lesson you are teaching. Leading up to the interview, I usually practice my lesson by acting it out. I usually do this on my own to practice the vocabulary and the order in which I want to deliver the lesson. Don't hesitate to have a plan by your side during the lesson for reference. I would recommend including as much information as possible in the lesson plan, so when you are nervous, you can refer to it and not forget anything.

Next, you'll want to prepare for the formal interview. It's worth browsing through the school's website to gather more information about the institution. Look into their school improvement plan and consider how your skills and knowledge align with it. Be prepared to explain why you applied to that specific school and why you are the right fit for the job. There are plenty of examples of interview questions and suggested answers available online. Take some time to think about your responses and reflect on your year: What have you achieved with your class? Which lessons are you particularly proud of?

Interview questions

1. Why do you want to work at this school? Or why did you decide to become a teacher? What is your teaching philosophy?
2. What can you bring to the school that will set you apart from the other candidates?
3. If I walked into your classroom, what would I see?
4. Can you tell me about a lesson that went well?
5. Can you tell me your strengths and weaknesses?
6. Tell me about a situation in which you had to deal with a pupil dysregulating.
7. What does behaviour management look like in your classroom?
8. Which behaviour management strategies have you found that are not effective and what has been effective?
9. How do you ensure you are developing as a teacher?
10. What are your career ambitions for the future?
11. Tell us about how you would teach the children about being safe?
12. What do you know about safeguarding?
13. How do you use ICT in your lessons?
14. Tell us about a time when you were concerned about a child e.g. neglect, trauma and what you did about it?
15. How would you value our church school ethos?
16. What do you know about current education news?
17. How would you support children with SEND?
18. Are you interested in leading a subject? If so, which subject would you be more confident in?
19. How do you cope with stress?
20. How will you engage reluctant learners?

Teaching_ with_ Mrs_ Aldridge

Even just being aware of what questions might come up can help. You will already be nervous in an interview, and you don't want to be more worried by an unfamiliar question. You don't have to make lots of notes for this process, just read some example interview questions and mentally bullet point your answers. This will hopefully help you feel more confident in the interview. It has worked for me.

You will always be asked if you have any questions at the end. It is a good idea to ask a question to show your interest and seize the opportunity to enquire about anything you're curious about or want to know regarding how things work at that school.

In my first-year interview, I asked about ECT support and how the school would support an ECT, including the process. You might want to ask any questions you didn't get the chance to ask on the tour. For example, you could ask about the school's vision for the upcoming year.

In my second year, I knew I wanted to lead a subject and be more involved across different year groups, so I asked about opportunities to lead a subject and contribute to whole school approaches. Another question could be about CPD opportunities at the school. If you'd like to know more about the staff working there, you could ask them what they love most about the school. They might mention when you will hear from them regarding the outcome of your application, but if they don't, you could politely enquire about the timeline. This is acceptable as you might have other commitments and wouldn't want to miss their call. Also, they might not call all candidates on the same day, so it's good to clarify.

I've had a few unsuccessful interviews, and finding out can be tough initially. It can be emotionally draining, but you have to keep trying. I always think that things happen for a reason, and there was obviously a reason I didn't get the job. With so many brilliant teachers out there, there's a lot of competition. Take some time to reflect and try to get feedback from the school, so you know what to work on for future interviews. Sometimes, it might be that you don't fit the school's specific needs.

In my first year, I was turned away from a job because they decided they didn't want an ECT due to building a whole new part of the school, which would have been a lot for them to take on. So, it's good to receive feedback and then move on, maintaining a positive outlook on the process.

If you were successful, don't start panicking and feeling the need to gather all the information about working there and prepare for September immediately. You will have plenty of new information and procedures to absorb, so take your time and don't overwhelm yourself. Take time to celebrate, as it's a significant achievement, and enjoy your summer before you start.

Following securing a teaching job, someone from HR will likely contact you within a week or so to fill out some forms. Once you've completed this process and your DBS check is complete, you will receive a letter of confirmation, and possibly your contract (sometimes the contract may not be provided until later in the summer). I would suggest discussing the school's transition day with someone there. It would be a great opportunity to meet your future class and some of the staff. The school might reach out to you about this, but if not, you can simply send a quick email to enquire. Then, you can check with your training provider or placement school if they will release you for that day (which they should).

Once you have the details, if you're working in a 2 or 3 form entry school, it would be worth speaking to the other teachers in the year group to plan for the transition day. As I mentioned earlier, every school does the transition differently. It's also a nice opportunity to have a conversation with the teacher(s) you'll be working with next year.

If you're going into EYFS, don't forget that you might have extra stay-and-play sessions, nursery visits, or a presentation evening for new parents. As someone going into EYFS, I found it helpful to arrange a meeting after school with the EYFS lead or other class teacher to discuss their approach.

You'll probably be eager to get into your classroom over the summer to set up, so it might be worth trying to visit your classroom before the school breaks up for summer. This will give you an idea of what you might need in your classroom, and you can consult the previous teacher to determine which resources belong to them and which ones will stay in the classroom. It's also important to find out if there are any non-negotiables for displays, as most schools have specific display requirements. Make sure to ask about this before you start setting up.

There are plenty of great classroom setup lists and ideas available online, on social media, and on Pinterest. Just make sure that what you're doing actually benefits the children, and don't spend too much time trying to make everything look perfect. Also, remember to use the summer to relax and recuperate. This is your holiday.

In the schools I've worked in, I didn't get my laptop or access to the curriculum or planning system until I started in September. I actually found this nice because it allowed me to enjoy my summer without feeling tempted to work excessively. You'll find that there's a lot of information when you start, but try to take it slowly and learn about the school and their processes bit by bit. Remember the concept of cognitive overload taught in our training and don't overwhelm yourself. Use the cognitive strategies you've learnt to gradually settle into the school.

I hope this chapter has been helpful and provided you with more awareness of the job process. I hope you feel less worried and can use my experiences and tips to assist you. I wish you luck in finding a job and remember to enjoy the process.

Here are the key takeaways for navigating the job process:

1. Seek advice from those around you.

2. Draft your personal statement ahead of time and adapt it when applying for a position.

3. Subscribe to job advertisement websites.

4. Schedule tours of schools, ask questions, and compliment the school.

5. Email questions about the class for your lesson observation to support planning.

6. Prepare for the formal interview by reviewing possible questions and practising your answers. Prepare a question to ask at the end.

7. Be confident and believe in yourself.

8. Remember that the job search process is challenging for everyone, and others are experiencing similar feelings. Keep trying, and you will eventually find success.

LESSON 8: BUILDING A STRONG TEACHER SUPPORT NETWORK

This was by far my favourite chapter to write and has been my favourite part of teaching: meeting so many fabulous teachers, some of whom will be lifelong friends. There's just a special bond between teachers that I don't think other people would completely understand. In this chapter, I'm going to explore a few reasons why it's great to have friends who are also teachers and to communicate with other colleagues.

FREE THERAPY

If you're having a difficult time, want some advice about a situation, or just want to have a general chat to know that you are not alone, talking to other teachers will really help. I love to talk, so that probably helps, but honestly, talking to other teachers is the best free therapy you'll ever have.

I have friends from my previous schools that I am still in touch with. Sometimes it's nice to chat about what's going on at work at the moment, get some things off your chest or out of your head, and talk to someone who has been through similar moments. Sometimes it's nice to just switch off from work completely and have a nice time with friends. Either way, whenever I speak to any other teachers, whether that be in my school or friends who are teachers, I instantly feel a sense of relief.

Meeting teachers in the printer room—it's like a mini therapy room, or if the printer's jammed, it can add even more stress to your day. It sounds funny, but honestly, this is the one place in school where you'll see teachers from all over the school. But in this moment, we all tend to talk about how our day or week is going, what's happening at school at the moment and how it makes us feel, and any upcoming events or meetings we need to think about. It seems like a good place to share feelings and know that you are not alone. I find that the things I was worried about in that moment are things that other teachers, no matter how much experience they have, also worry about, such as upcoming parents' evenings, report deadlines, assessments, and planning. We all experience these, and it's nice to have a chat, especially with some people you rarely get to spend time with.

Staff meetings and training days are another good time to talk to other teachers. It's a nice opportunity to share the good and the bad from our week. I particularly like it when we share good moments and achievements from our classes, something funny a child has said that week, a strategy that worked really well, or behaviour management advice from the week. Although everyone is usually tired from their busy days, it's still nice to get together and share practices.

You will probably build a good relationship with the other teacher(s) in your year group or maybe key stage if you are in a one-form-entry school. Something you might find yourself doing or notice other people doing is going into the other person's classroom. Usually, you start chatting, and then you find yourself sitting on the side of a desk or on a tiny little chair, chatting away and not getting much work done. I reckon over my first two years of teaching, I have done this a lot of times! It's just a nice way to share how your day went, compare different activities to see how the other class got on with them, and I find that I go home feeling a lot better after that. It's not usually a long chat, as teachers always have lots of other work to do, but it's like a mini reflection of the day. Some people might have more discipline and just stay in their own bubble and continue working, but I think it's quite nice to share how our days went and discuss planning for the following day.

I understand that everyone is different, so you might not like to talk as much as me, but trust me, try it and see how it makes you feel. You don't have to do this every day or every week, but if you are feeling overwhelmed or even want to share something positive that has happened, do it. You'll find that it'll probably make you and the other person feel better. You don't need to talk about your feelings in depth, just have a quick chat so you know that you are not alone.

66

TEACHERS NEED OTHER
TEACHERS. THIS IS NOT A
JOB THAT CAN BE DONE
ALONE. COLLABORATION
AND FRIENDSHIP ARE VITAL
IN KEEPING TEACHERS
SANE AND HAPPY.

Teresa Kwant

SHARE IDEAS AND EXPERIENCES

Who better to learn from than other teachers, especially when you're in your first few years of teaching? Situations might come up that you have never dealt with before: a query from a parent you are not sure how to respond to, teaching a concept you are not familiar with, getting your head around a new school and its policies and procedures. There will be a lot of new experiences for you, and it is good to learn from other teachers.

During your first two years, you will have a mentor. Your weekly meetings will consist of discussing different aspects of teaching and strategies, giving you a chance to learn new things and ask questions. Your mentor will also drop in to observe your lessons, providing valuable feedback. If you are unsure how to break down a concept for teaching, just ask your mentor for advice. The extended two-year mentorship program is designed to give you the opportunity to learn from others and build a support network.

I mentioned this in lesson 5, but you will gain ideas from observing other teachers. Especially in your first year, try to observe another teacher every week during your ECT (Early Career

Teacher) time. You don't need to stay for a whole lesson, just pop in, have a look for something new to try out with your class, examine their students' work, and talk to the children. You can even learn from other year groups and key stages, adapting strategies to suit your own class. Exposing yourself to all of this will make you a better teacher and provide you with a wealth of knowledge and ideas to try out.

Shared experiences will bring you closer to other teachers. In my first year, I worked at a school camp during some of the holidays. There were various staff members, but quite a few of them were teachers. I met a fellow teacher who also worked in the same year group as me. We have now become good friends and meet up regularly, even though we don't work together at the camp anymore. Sharing the experience of being an Early Years teacher brought us closer. The first time we met up after the camp, we talked for hours, and the staff at the coffee shop had to ask us to leave as they were tidying up. I don't think either of us realised how long we had been talking.

We shared so many ideas, feelings, and experiences. We discussed situations that had occurred and offered each other advice. We talked about different strategies we had tried and things we had seen other teachers do. Although the fact that we are both teachers brought us together, we also talk about things other than work, and it's nice to take a break from that too. I remember her mentioning that their school was looking to change their behaviour policy and they were asked to find different ideas to present to the headteacher. We were able to discuss what I had experienced in my previous schools, and she had lots of ideas that she took back to her school. The best way to discover something new is through sharing practices.

KNOWLEDGE IS POWER. KNOWLEDGE SHARED IS POWER MULTIPLIED.

ROBERT BOYCE

SHARED UNDERSTANDING OF THE PROFESSION

Teaching is a truly unique profession that requires immense passion and strength. As teachers, we have a deep-rooted commitment to our students' happiness, success, and personal growth. However, this dedication comes with a lot of hard work.

Despite the common misconception of teachers having short workdays and extended holidays, we know that our job extends far beyond those hours. We have numerous responsibilities and tasks to fulfil outside of classroom time. Often, we find ourselves working during holidays, investing our personal time and effort without monetary compensation. This aspect of our profession may not be widely understood by those outside the teaching community. It's important to be surrounded by colleagues who comprehend the realities of our work.

In this section, we are reminded of the significance of teacher friends and why they play a crucial role in our lives. They understand our experiences and challenges better than anyone else possibly could. It's vital to reflect on the initial reasons that motivated us to become teachers and recognise the positive impact we have made on our students' lives. While we tirelessly juggle various responsibilities and wear multiple hats to provide the best for our children, it's equally essential to prioritise self-care and look after ourselves.

Teaching is a rewarding yet demanding profession, and having teacher friends who truly understand the joys and struggles can be an invaluable source of support and understanding.

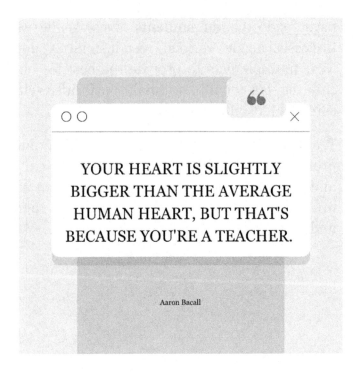

YOUR HEART IS SLIGHTLY
BIGGER THAN THE AVERAGE
HUMAN HEART, BUT THAT'S
BECAUSE YOU'RE A TEACHER.

Aaron Bacall

TEACHER RESOURCES

Social media has become an integral part of society, and for teachers, it offers a valuable platform to connect with other educators, share ideas, and exchange experiences.

The online teacher community is vast, and you can find specific groups tailored to your needs, such as year groups, locations, Early Career Teacher (ECT) groups, and subject leadership groups. The wealth of knowledge available at your fingertips is truly remarkable.

Take some time to explore and join groups that align with your interests and areas of support. What do you need assistance with? What experiences can you share with others? As an ECT, there are countless teachers out there willing to offer support. People seek advice on setting up their first classrooms, transition activities, job applications, and lesson observation ideas for interviews, among many other topics. If you have a question or curiosity about something, browse online, and you're likely to find the answer. And if you don't, don't hesitate to ask—teachers are incredibly supportive, and there's always someone willing to help.

Social media platforms also offer a wealth of

ideas for classroom setup and activities. While planning, don't feel pressured to create everything from scratch. Utilise the resources available to you. Many websites provide examples of planning, both short-term and long-term, along with specific lesson plans and activities. Don't be afraid to use and adapt existing documents to suit your needs.

In addition to specific support, online platforms offer a sense of general support. If you're facing behavioural challenges in your classroom and are unsure how to address them, there are teachers out there ready to provide ideas and advice. Teaching is a profession that constantly evolves, so feel confident in exploring new ideas and experimenting with different approaches.

Reading various teaching books is another excellent way to enhance your practice. Research-based books, memoirs, biographies— there are numerous options available to support you as a professional. Many schools have CPD libraries with teaching books that you can borrow and return.

Although teaching is a demanding job and time may be limited, I highly recommend finding moments to read. Even if it's just 10 minutes a day or an hour a week, dedicate time to gain new ideas and learn from others' experiences.

Having personally read several teaching books and finding them immensely helpful, I felt compelled to write a book myself to support other teachers and share my experiences. If writing this book allows me to reach just one teacher and provide them with valuable advice, I will consider it a success.

Teaching requires significant dedication, but it's important to continually work on expanding your knowledge and cultivating a support network that empowers you.

IN THE CASE OF GOOD BOOKS, THE POINT IS NOT TO SEE HOW MANY OF THEM YOU CAN GET THROUGH, BUT RATHER HOW MANY CAN GET TO YOU.

@WEARETEACHERS

EPILOGUE: A FINAL MESSAGE FROM ME

I really hope you have found my book helpful and that it has provided you with some different ideas and resources to assist you as an Early Career Teacher. Entering the world of teaching with only a small idea of what to expect can be daunting, so I hope that I have alleviated some of this pressure for you.

I have tried to address some of the main hurdles I came across, offering my lessons and honest feelings about certain situations. I want you to know that the emotions you will experience in your first few years are normal, and you will have both good days and bad days.

My main piece of advice would be to focus on the positive. Look for something positive every day and practice gratitude. While I encourage you to reflect and discuss the challenges with others, try not to get too caught up in negativity.

You will have countless lovely moments with your students, so take the time to appreciate them. I wish you all the best in your teaching journey.

RESOURCES

You can scan the QR codes below to be instantly directed to my TES account where you can download resource templates shown in this book and access my teaching social media account.

I am always happy to chat with people and offer support. I would also love to hear about your achievements and experiences.

 Instagram:

teaching_with_mrs_aldridge

 TES:

Teaching_with_Mrs_Aldridge

REFERENCES

Bacall, A. (2023) Country living; 35 Teacher Quotes to Thank the Inspirational Educators you Know. Available at: https://www.countryliving.com/life/inspirational-stories/g33930560/teacher-quotes/ (Accessed on: 10th July 2023)

Boyce, R. (2023) Inspiring quotes. Available at: https://www.inspiringquotes.us/quotes/kwl7_WjT YXyLz (Accessed on: 10th July)

Covey, Stephen R. (2009). The 7 Habits of Highly Effective People (Kindle). RosettaBooks - A. Kindle Edition.

Department for Education (DfE) (2019) Early Career Framework. Available at https://www.gov.uk/government/publications/early-career-framework (Accessed: 9th July 2023).

Dix, P. (2017) When the adults change, everything changes. Independendent Thinking Press.

Kwant, T. (2023) Teresa Kwant, inspiring idea for elementary educators. Available at: https://teresakwant.com/ (Accessed: 9th July 2023)

We are Teachers (2023) We are teachers; 50 of our favourite quotes about reading. Available at: https://www.weareteachers.com/quotes-about-reading/ (Accessed on 10th July 2023)

Printed in Great Britain
by Amazon

28634657R00076